Hide and Seek

Jane Thompson and Stephen Thompson

Pupil's Book 3

CENGAGE Learning

Australia • Brazil • Mexico • Singapore • United Kingdom • United States

Hide and Seek 3 Scope and sequence

Unit	Topic	Structures	Lexis and phrases	Functions	Phonics and literacy	Numbers	Maths	Our world	Values	Art
1	Back to school! (Revision)	How are you? I'm fine, thank you. Who's here? I am ... I can/can't ... Do you want to ... ? Do you have ... ? I have/don't have ... I want to ... There's/There isn't Where is/are ... ? ... has got ...	Hello, Goodbye, and, but, children, everyone, bat, ball, play, happy, sad, good, pen, pot, table, book, cup, clock, window, door, tail, bug, spots, butterfly, wings, frog, fish, rabbit, horse	Greetings Answer and ask questions	Review: alphabet Review: Level 2 phonics	Review: 0–20	Review: positional vocabulary: in, on under, above, in front of, behind, next to, between	Abilities and movement: *walk, fly, jump, skip, roll, bounce, slide, climb, move* Describing people: hair, eye colour	Good homework habits	Make a book about you
2	What day is it today?	What day is it today? Can you spell ... ? What page, please?	page, line, spell, reading, lesson, Monday, Tuesday, Wednesday, Thursday, Friday, Saturday, Sunday, tomorrow, yesterday, afternoon, morning	Ask simple questions related to English lessons Ask what day it is	oo book/zoo th three/this	10 20 Count in tens to 20 Understand 20 as two lots of 10	Days of the week Describe the passage of time	Observations about animal routines	Keep school work neat	Make a book about school
3	How we travel	I come to school by ... I ... at ... o'clock. What time is it? How many more? Most children come to school by ...	near, far away, road, taxi, metro, rails, float, travel (on), push, bike, wind, wheel, sail, pedal, wear, helmet, seat belt	Make statements about routine actions	ar car oa boat	30 40 Count in tens to 40 Understand 30 and 40 as 3 and 4 lots of 10	Tell the time: o' clock Identify the time of routine events	What cars, boats and trains move on Investigate *push* and movement	Be safe outside	Make a model vehicle
4	Let's keep warm and dry!	What is he/she wearing? Who's wearing ... ?	scarf, gloves, jumper, pink, purple, orange, raincoat, boot, sandal, shoe, warm, clothes	Describe clothes and colours Answer questions with *wearing*	ng swing ai paint	50 Count in tens to 50 Understand 50 as 5 lots of 10 Count to and back from 50 in tens	Comparisons of three objects: the longest, the shortest, the heaviest, the lightest	Textiles and their properties: warm and cool Mixing primary colours	Dress yourself	Make a shoe-lace card
5	People who help us	What's his/her/their job? What do you want for lunch? Today is ... Yesterday was ...	cook, job, lunch, doctor, bus driver, vet, footballer, runner, tennis player, baker, oven, shop, school cleaner, security man	Ask questions related to jobs	ch chip er teacher	60 70 Count in tens to 70 Understand 60 and 70 as 6 and 7 lots of 10	Comparison of size: *taller, tallest, shorter, shortest* Recognise the position of objects: above, below	Vets and care of animals Processes: baking bread	Ways to be helpful to others	Make a thank-you card

Unit	Topic	Structures	Lexis and phrases	Functions	Phonics and literacy	Numbers	Maths	Our world	Values	Art
6	What's wrong?	Can I have ... ? What's wrong? I feel ill. My (tummy) hurts. Don't worry. It isn't fair! How many more? I/You need ... He/She needs ...	cheese, hungry, thirsty, tummy, hurts, (not) enough, upset, sleepy, lonely, mean, doctor, alive, living thing	Ask about feelings	ee feet air hair	80 90 Count in tens to 90 Understand 80 and 90 as 8 and 9 lots of 10	Understand when there is not enough of something	Look after our bodies Living and non-living things	Be kind to others	Make a friendship poster
7	How do things feel?	What does ... feel like? It feels/They feel ... It looks/They look ... Show me something (rough).	brush, shelf, feel, sticky, rough, smooth, spines, shell, thick, hairy, nails, iron (n), burn (v), knife, cut (v)	Describe the physical properties of objects and animals	sh fish ur fur	100 Understand 100 as ten lots of ten Count to and back from 100 in tens	3D shapes and properties: cone, sphere, tube, cube, cuboid, corners, edges, faces, curved, flat, round	Talk about properties of fur, shell, spines Animal features and properties: teeth, claws, fingers	Be safe in the kitchen	Make a monster
8	Same and different	Which is your ... ? It's the (little) one. What do they find? Do they find (treasure)? They're the same/a different shape/size/colour. How many are left?	flag, treasure, spade, dig, beach, starfish, crab, lobster, beak, neck, gull, flamingo, rocks	Identify possessions	oi point ure treasure	Count on and back in tens Simple subtraction from 10	Identify how objects are the same or different: colour, size, shape	Animals on the seashore Know that materials can change: wet and dry sand	Think of others on the beach	Make an underwater picture
9	How animals help us	What do they do on the farm? We get (eggs) from (hens). (Cows) give us (milk). Count (all) the ...	hen, egg, milk (v), wife, barn, hay, inside, outside, afterwards, shelter, medicine, healthy	Talk about where food comes from	ow cow or horse	Doubling numbers (to 10)	Comparative volume of liquid: full, half-full, empty	Farm animals and what they give us: milk, wool, eggs Objects that float and sink	Look after animals	Make a farmyard picture
10	Everyday routines	Before I ... I ... After I ... I ... What happens at (10) o'clock? When's lunch? It can't be time (for bed) yet.	get washed/dressed, sometimes, visit, supper, Goodnight, lunchtime, active, clean your teeth, toothbrush, toothpaste, smile, late, on time	Talk about routines	ear ear igh night	Consolidate counting to and back from 100 in tens Consolidate doubling numbers (to 10)	Telling the time: hours	Keeping fit: active vs inactive pastimes Good dental health	Be on time	Make a name poster

Unit 1 · Lesson 1

Together again!

Key language:
(Greetings); Who's here?; Is (Sam) here?; I can/can't see ... ; and; but; children; everyone

- Warm up **1.2**
- Letters review: *a–z*
- Rhyme: *Alphabet* [*a–z*] **1.3**
- Look, listen and read. **1.4**
- Game: *Roleplay*
- Rhyme: *Goodbye* **1.5**

Unit 1 • Lesson 2

Time to play!

Key language:
bat; ball; play; I have/don't have a ... ; Do you have a ... ?; What's wrong?; I'm sorry.

- Warm up
- Letters and sounds: *s, a, t, p, i, n* **1.6**
- Rhyme: *Come and play* **1.7**
- Look, listen and read. **1.8**
- Game: *What's wrong?*
- Rhyme: *The sun has got his hat on!* **1.9**

Unit 1 • Lesson 3

Spot the difference

Key language:
Zero–ten; There is/isn't a ... ; in; on; under; above; in front of; behind; next to; between; Where is/are ... ?

- Warm up
- Hide and seek: *0, 1*
- Rhyme: *Numbers* [to *10*] **1.10**
- Read, listen and say. **1.11**
- Game: *Where is it?*
- Rhyme: *Five little cakes* **1.12**

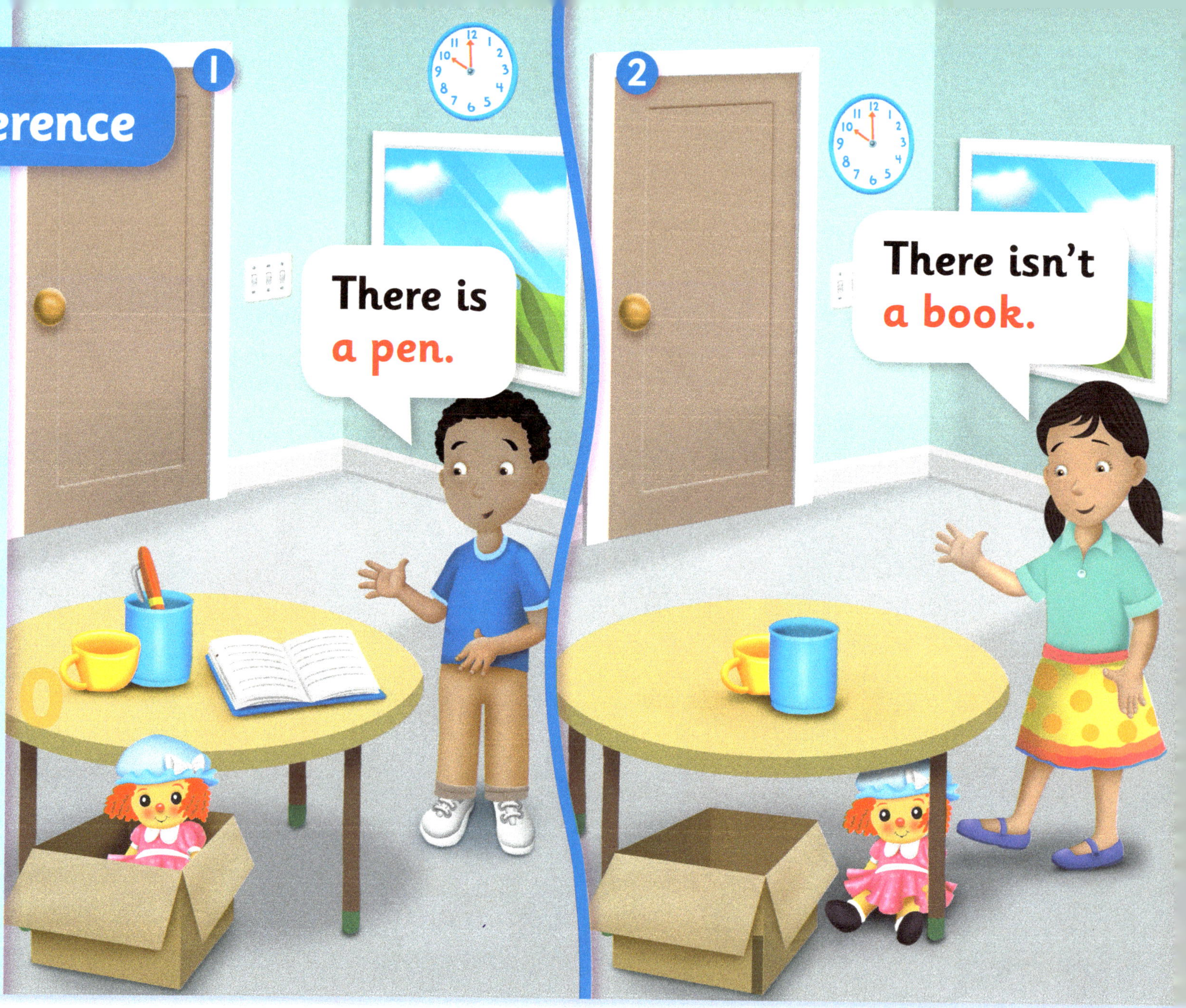

0 1 2 3 4 5

Unit 1 • Lesson 4

How many can you find?

Key language:
ten–twenty; tail; legs; bug; spots; butterfly; wings; red; blue; yellow; black

- Warm up
- Hide and seek: *11, 13, 15*
- Rhyme: *My body (V1–2)* **1.13**
- Read, listen and count. **1.14**
- Game: *Robot says*
- Rhyme: *One, two. How are you?* [to *20*] **1.15**

6 7 8 9 10

Unit 1 · Lesson 5
Let's move!

Key language:
fish; rabbit; horse; swim; jump; skip; run

- Warm up
- Letters and sounds: *m, d, g, o, e* 1.16
- Rhyme: *Our world* 1.17
- Read, listen and stick. 1.18
- Game: *Start and stop!*
- Rhyme: *A monkey can climb.* 1.19

1

Fish can ______.

2

Rabbits can ______.

3

Horses can ______.

4

Children can ______.

Unit 1 • Lesson 6

Who is this?

Key language:
She/He has long/short hair.; Her/His eyes are blue/brown.

- Warm up
- Letters and sounds: *c, k, (ck), u, r, h* **1.20**
- Rhyme: *Our world* **1.17**
- Read, listen and stick. **1.21**
- Game: *Who's missing?*
- Rhyme: *Colours (V1–2)* **1.22**

This is [ ] .

This is [ ] .

This is [ ] .

This is [ ] .

Unit 1 • Lesson 7

Homework time!

Key language:
I can read/write.; homework; work (v); watch; TV; too; Mum; Dad; help (v)

- Warm up
- Reading
- Rhyme: *Values* **1.23**
- Read, listen and draw. **1.24**
- Game: *This is my friend.*
- Rhyme: *Choose*

I do my homework.

1

Mum and Dad help me.

2

The TV is on.

Unit 1 • Lesson 8

A book about me!

1

2

Key language:
fold; tear

- Warm up
- Spelling
- Rhyme: *Art* 1.26
- Watch and draw.
- Game: *Choose*
- Rhyme: *Goodbye* 1.5

3

4

Unit 2 · Lesson 1

Can you read?

Key language:
book; zoo; page; line; reading; Monday; lesson

- Warm up
- Seek and say: *oo* **1.27**
- Rhyme: *Letters and sounds* **1.28**
- Look, listen and say. **1.29**
- Game: *Missing words*
- Rhyme: *The zoo* **1.30**

oo

Unit 2 • Lesson 2

Can you spell?

Key language:
three; this; Tuesday; word; spelling; thin; last

- Warm up
- Seek and say: *th* **1.31**
- Rhyme: *Sounds* **1.32**
- Look, listen and say. **1.33**
- Game: *Rhyming words*
- Rhyme: *Sound out words* **1.34**

Unit 2 · Lesson 3

Morning and afternoon

Key language:
Wednesday; Thursday; morning; afternoon; yesterday was ... ; maths; spell

- Warm up
- Hide and seek: *10* **1.35**
- Rhyme: *Ten little children* **1.36**
- Listen and stick. **1.37**
- Game: *Bingo!*
- Rhyme: *Coming to school (V1)* **1.38**

1

2

10

0 10 20 30 40 50

My snacks

Key language:
Friday; Saturday; Sunday; tomorrow

- Warm up
- Hide and seek: *20* 1.39
- Rhyme: *Twenty legs* 1.40
- Listen and match. 1.41
- Game: *A story about days*
- Rhyme: *Days of the week* 1.42

20

Unit 2 • Lesson 5

In the morning ...

Key language:
rest; look for food

- Warm up
- Letters and sounds
- Rhyme: *Our world* 1.17
- Read, listen and match. 1.43
- Game: *Today is ...*
- Rhyme: *Days of the week* 1.42

I rest in the sun.

1

2

I sit in my pool.

I look for food.

3

In the evening ...

Key language:
evening; desert; moth; racoon; fox

- Warm up
- Letters and sounds
- Rhyme: *Our world* **1.17**
- Read, listen and stick. **1.44**
- Game: *Animal mime*
- Rhyme: *Goodnight!* **1.45**

1

This is a ________.

2

This is a ________.

3

This is a ________.

Unit 2 · Lesson 7

Neat and clean

Key language:
neat

- Warm up
- Reading
- Rhyme: *Values* **1.23**
- Read and circle.
- Game: *Stop the clock!*
- Rhyme: *Choose*

My school things are neat.

Is this neat?

yes no

yes no

Unit 2 · Lesson 8

My book about school

1

2

Key language:
read; play; snack; home; fold; art

- Warm up
- Spelling
- Rhyme: *Art* **1.26**
- Make, write and draw.
- Game: *Choose*
- Rhyme: *Goodbye* **1.5**

3

4

Unit 3 · Lesson 1

Coming to school

Key language:
car; near; far away

- Warm up
- Seek and say: *ar* 1.46
- Rhyme: *Letters and sounds* 1.28
- Read, listen and stick. 1.47
- Game: *Roleplay*
- Rhyme: *The wheels on the bus* 1.48

ar

Unit 3 • Lesson 2

Let's go to the park!

Key language:
boat; road; ride (v); I won't!

- Warm up
- Seek and say: *oa* 1.49
- Rhyme: *Sounds* 1.32
- Listen, read and answer. 1.50
- Game: *Reading pairs*
- Rhyme: *Row your boat.* 1.51

oa

Unit 3 · Lesson 3

How many?

Key language: *thirty; (the) most; taxi; metro; on foot*

- Warm up
- Hide and seek: *30* **1.52**
- Rhyme: *Two, four, six, eight* **1.53**
- Listen, stick and count. **1.54**
- Game: *Class survey*
- Rhyme: *Coming to school (V1–2)* **1.55**

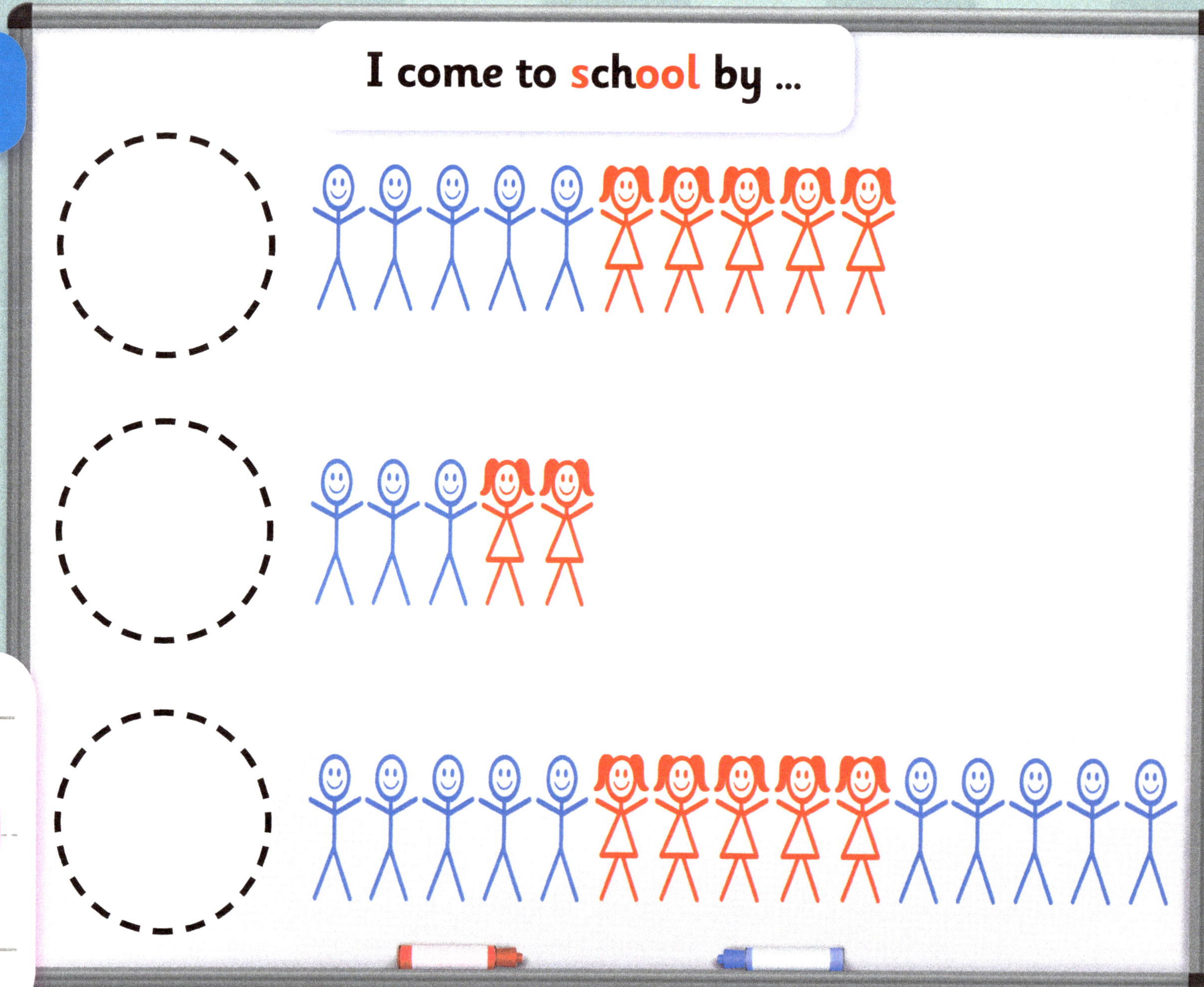

30

Unit 3 · Lesson 4

It's time to ...

Key language: *forty; clock; o'clock; What's the time?; It's ... ; time to (get up)*

- Warm up
- Hide and seek: *40* **1.56**
- Rhyme: *I can count in tens!* [to *40*] **1.57**
- Listen, read and write. **1.58**
- Game and Rhyme: *Hickory, dickory dock* **1.59**
- Rhyme: *Hop round the clock!* **1.60**

I get up at ____ o'clock.

School starts at ____ o'clock.

I have lunch at ____ o'clock.

I go to bed at ____ o'clock.

40

60 70 80 90 100

Unit 3 · Lesson 5

What does it go on?

Key language:
rails; float; travel

- Warm up
- Letters and sounds
- Rhyme: *Our world* 1.17
- Read, listen and stick. 1.61
- Game: *Start and stop*
- Rhyme: *Coming to school* (*V1–2*) 1.55

1

Cars go on the road.

2

Trains go on rails.

3

Boats float on water.

Unit 3 · Lesson 6

What makes them move?

Key language: *water wheel; move; sail; pedal*

- Warm up
- Letters and sounds
- Rhyme: *Our world* 1.17
- Read, listen and circle. 1.62
- Game: *Picture and word pairs*
- Rhyme: *Push it away!* 1.63

1

This is my bike.

2

This is a water wheel.

3

This boat has a sail.

Unit 3 • Lesson 7

Be safe!

Key language:
wear; helmet; seat belt

- Warm up
- Reading
- Rhyme: *Values* **1.23**
- Read and choose.
- Game: *Stop the clock!*
- Rhyme: *Choose*

I am safe.

My car

Key language:
model

- Warm up
- Spelling
- Rhyme: *Art* **1.26**
- Watch and make.
- Game: *Choose*
- Rhyme: *The wheels on the bus* **1.48**

1

2

3

4

Unit 4 • Lesson 1

It's cold today

Key language:
swing; gloves; scarf; jumper; pink; purple

- Warm up
- Seek and say: *ng* **1.64**
- Rhyme: *Letters and sounds* **1.28**
- Read, listen and stick. **1.65**
- Game: *Dressing-up race*
- Rhyme: *The sun comes up.* **1.66**

Unit 4 · Lesson 2

It's raining!

Key language:
paint; raincoat; boots; orange; little

- Warm up
- Seek and say: *ai* **1.67**
- Rhyme: *Sounds* **1.32**
- Read, listen and match. **1.68**
- Game: *This is my friend.*
- Rhyme: *Incy Wincy spider* **1.69**

ai

Unit 4 · Lesson 3

The longest scarf

Key language:
fifty; (the) longest; (the) shortest

- Warm up
- Hide and seek: *50* **1.70**
- Rhyme: *I can count in tens!* [to *50*] **1.71**
- Read, listen and match. **1.72**
- Game: *Guess how long!*
- Rhyme: *Hop round the clock!* **1.60**

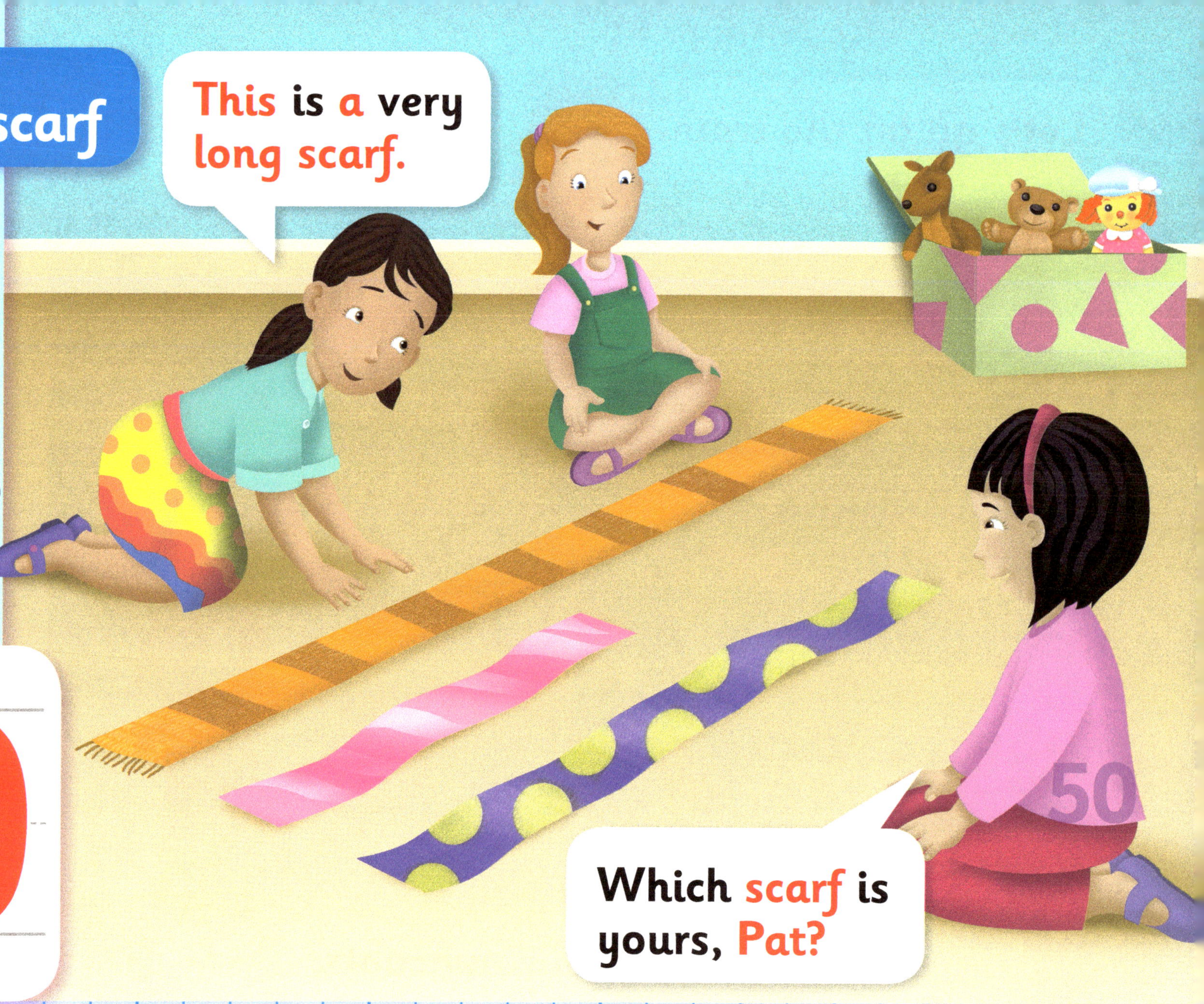

50

0 10 20 30 40 50

Unit 4 · Lesson 4

Which is the heaviest?

Key language:
(the) heaviest; (the) lightest; shoe; sandal

- Warm up
- Hide and seek: *10s*
- Rhyme: *I count back in tens.* [from *50*] **1.73**
- Listen and match. **1.74**
- Game: *Animal parade*
- Rhyme: *Are you heavier?* **1.75**

Unit 4 · Lesson 5

Warm and cool

Key language:
cotton; warm; (the) warmest; clothes

- Warm up
- Letters and sounds
- Rhyme: *Our world* 1.17
- Read, listen and answer. 1.76
- Game: *Kim's game*
- Rhyme: *Point to your clothes (V1–2)* 1.77

1

2

3

Mixing colours

Key language:
mix; What colour does it make?; It makes ...

- Warm up
- Letters and sounds
- Rhyme: *Our world* **1.17**
- Read, listen and stick. **1.78**
- Game: *This is my friend.*
- Rhyme: *Colours (V1–3)* **2.2**

 +  =

Red and yellow make ___ ?

 +  =

Yellow and blue make ___ ?

 +  =

Blue and red make ___ ?

Unit 4 • Lesson 7

Yes, I can!

Key language:
dress (v); himself/myself; try

- Warm up
- Reading
- Rhyme: *Values* **1.23**
- Read and choose.
- Game: *Stop the clock!*
- Rhyme: *Time to get dressed!* **2.3**

I can dress myself.

Pam's mum dresses her.

Tom can dress himself.

A lacing card

1

2

Key language:
shoe; lace; tight

- Warm up
- Spelling
- Rhyme: *Art* **1.26**
- Colour and tie.
- Game: *Choose*
- Rhyme: *Goodbye* **1.5**

3

4

Unit 5 · Lesson 1

Mrs Chaplin

Key language:
chip; cook (n); lunch; What's her job?

- Warm up
- Seek and say: *ch* **2.4**
- Rhyme: *Letters and sounds* **1.28**
- Read, listen and draw. **2.5**
- Game: *Missing words*
- Rhyme: *It's 12 o'clock.* **2.6**

ch

Unit 5 · Lesson 2
Sam's book

Key language:
teacher; doctor; bus driver; What are their jobs?

- Warm up
- Seek and say: *er* **2.7**
- Rhyme: *Sounds* **1.32**
- Read, listen and answer. **2.8**
- Game: *Rhyming words*
- Rhyme: *A teacher in a school* **2.9**

er

Unit 5 · Lesson 3

Who's the tallest?

Key language:
sixty; (the) tallest; tennis player; footballer; runner

- Warm up
- Hide and seek: *60* **2.10**
- Rhyme: *I can count in tens!* [to *60*] **2.11**
- Listen and stick. **2.12**
- Game: *Sizes*
- Rhyme: *Are you taller?* **2.13**

60

[ ] is a tennis player.

[ ] is a footballer.

[ ] is a runner.

0 10 20 30 40 50

Unit 5 • Lesson 4

Below and above

Key language:
seventy; above; below

- Warm up
- Hide and seek: *70* **2.14**
- Rhyme: *I count back in tens.* [from *70*] **2.15**
- Listen and circle. **2.16**
- Game: *Memory game*
- Rhyme: *Days of the week* **1.42**

70

60 70 80 90 100

Unit 5 · Lesson 5

Vets help

Key language:
sick; vet; pet; Vets help ...

- Warm up
- Letters and sounds
- Rhyme: *Our world* **1.17**
- Read, listen and match. **2.17**
- Game: *Animal snap!*
- Rhyme: *Uncle Ali has a farm.* **2.18**

Vets help farm animals, too.

1 2 3

Vets help sick animals.

Vets help pets.

Unit 5 · Lesson 6

Bakers help us

Key language:
baker; shop; busy; bake; oven; ready; cool; sells

- Warm up
- Letters and sounds
- Rhyme: *Our world* **1.17**
- Read, listen and match. **2.19** and **2.20**
- Game: *Cloud game*
- Rhyme: *Pat-a-cake* **2.21**

First

Then

Next

Last

Unit 5 • Lesson 7

I help, too!

Key language:
helpful; on time; litter

- Warm up
- Reading
- Rhyme: *Values* **1.23**
- Look, read and say.
- Game: *Stop the clock!*
- Rhyme: *Please and thank you* **2.22**

I am helpful.

Be polite.
Be on time.
Don't drop litter.

Unit 5 · Lesson 8

A thank-you card

1

2

3

4

Key language:
(school) cleaner; security man; maid

- Warm up
- Spelling
- Rhyme: *Art* **1.26**
- Listen, make and write.
- Game: *Choose*
- Rhyme: *A teacher in a school* **2.9**

Unit 6 • Lesson 1

Are you hungry?

Key language:
feet; cheese; hungry; thirsty; Can I have ... ?

- Warm up
- Seek and say: *ee* **2.23**
- Rhyme: *Letters and sounds* **1.28**
- Listen, answer and read. **2.24**
- Game: *Roleplay*
- Rhyme: *If you're happy and you know it, ...* **2.25**

ee

Unit 6 • Lesson 2

What's wrong?

Key language:
hair; I feel ill.; tummy; ... hurts; What's wrong?; Don't worry.

- Warm up
- Seek and say: *air* **2.26**
- Rhyme: *Sounds* **1.32**
- Listen, read and stick. **2.27**
- Game: *Robot says*
- Rhyme: *Miss Polly has a dolly.* **2.28**

air

Unit 6 · Lesson 3

Not enough bananas!

Key language: *eighty; It isn't fair!; (not) enough; upset*

- Warm up
- Hide and seek: *80* **2.29**
- Rhyme: *I can count in tens!* [to *80*] **2.30**
- Listen and answer. **2.31**
- Game: *Disappearing mats*
- Rhyme: *The sun has got his hat on!* **1.9**

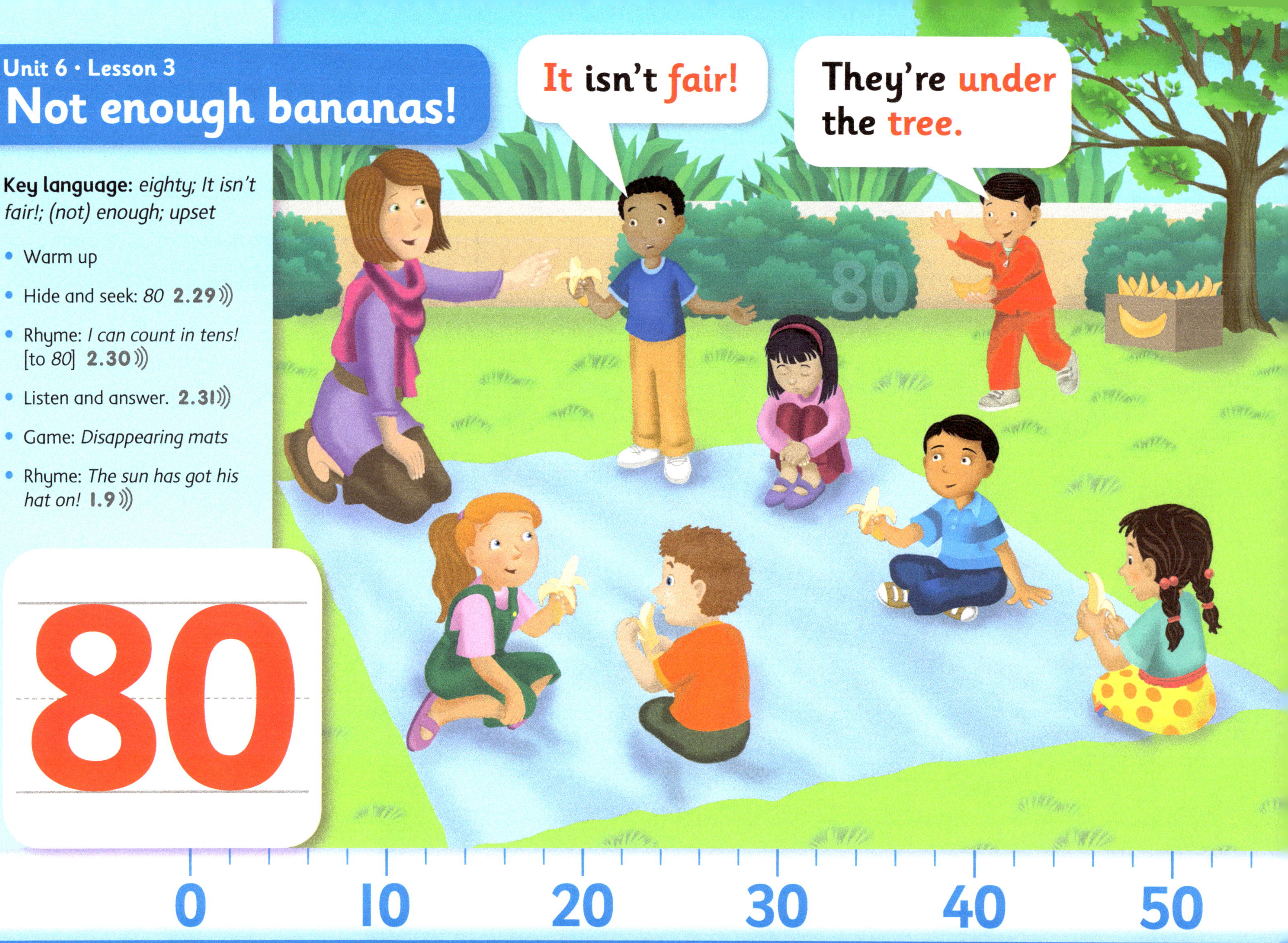

Unit 6 • Lesson 4

How many more?

Key language:
ninety; How many more?

- Warm up
- Hide and seek: 90 **2.32**
- Rhyme: *I count back in tens.* [from 90] **2.33**
- Listen and stick. **2.34**
- Game: *How many more?*
- Rhyme: *Ten little children* **1.36**

90

60 70 80 90 100

Unit 6 • Lesson 5

Look after your body

Key language:
sleepy; I need … . He/She needs … .

- Warm up
- Letters and sounds
- Rhyme: *Our world* **1.17**
- Listen and match. **2.35**
- Game: *How do you feel?*
- Rhyme: *If I bump my head, … .* **2.36**

1

2

3

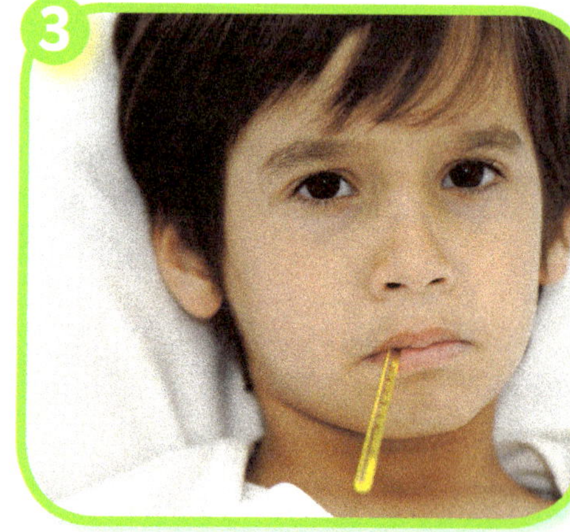

You need … .

a drink

a doctor

to sleep

Unit 6 · Lesson 6
Is it living?

Key language:
alive; living (thing); Is it living?

- Warm up
- Letters and sounds
- Rhyme: *Our world* **1.17**
- Look, read and circle.
- Game: *Vote*
- Rhyme: *Head, shoulders, knees and toes* **2.37**

a plant   yes   no

a chair   yes   no

a cat   yes   no

a train   yes   no

Unit 6 • Lesson 7

Look after others

Key language:
lonely; mean (unkind)

- Warm up
- Reading
- Rhyme: *Values* **1.23**
- Say, listen and draw. **2.38**
- Game: *Stop the clock!*
- Rhyme: *Good friends* **2.39**

I look after others.

Unit 6 • Lesson 8

A friendship poster

1

2

Key language:
friendship poster

- Warm up
- Spelling
- Rhyme: *Art* **1.26**
- Draw and colour.
- Game: *Choose*
- Rhyme: *Good friends* **2.39**

3

4

Unit 7 · Lesson 1

Sticky hands

Key language:
fish; sticky; feel; brush; shelf

- Warm up
- Seek and say: *sh* **2.40**
- Rhyme: *Letters and sounds* **1.28**
- Read and listen. **2.41**
- Game: *Mime*
- Rhyme: *Wash (V1–3)* **2.42**

sh

Unit 7 · Lesson 2
What does it feel like?

Key language:
fur; smooth; rough

- Warm up
- Seek and say: *ur* **2.43**
- Rhyme: *Sounds* **1.32**
- Read, listen and answer. **2.44**
- Game: *Start and stop*
- Rhyme: *Textures (V1)* **2.45**

Unit 7 · Lesson 3

Make 10

Key language:
one hundred; hop (n); How many more to make ten?

- Warm up
- Hide and seek: *100* **2.46**
- Rhyme: *I can count in tens!* [to *100*] **2.47**
- Count and match.
- Game: *Find your partner.*
- Rhyme: *Ten green bottles* **2.48**

Unit 7 · Lesson 4

What is it?

Key language:
cone; point; round; sphere; cylinder

- Warm up
- Hide and seek: *Shapes*
- Rhyme: *I count back in tens.* [from *100*] **2.49**
- Listen and stick. **2.50**
- Game: *What's in the bag?*
- Rhyme: *Shapes (V1–4)* **2.51**

Unit 7 · Lesson 5

Animal coats

Key language:
shell; spines; thick

- Warm up
- Letters and sounds
- Rhyme: *Our world* **1.17**
- Listen and stick. **2.52**
- Game: *Touch and guess!*
- Rhyme: *Shamlar the camel* **2.53**

1

2

3

Unit 7 · Lesson 6
Whose is it?

Key language:
hairy; nails; claws; teeth

- Warm up
- Letters and sounds
- Rhyme: *Our world* **1.17**
- Read, listen and match. **2.54**
- Game: *Questions*
- Rhyme: *Textures (V1–2)* **2.55**

1

2

3

chimp

shark

falcon

Unit 7 • Lesson 7

Don't touch!

Key language:
burn (v); iron; knife; cut (v); Don't touch!; Why not?

- Warm up
- Reading
- Rhyme: *Values* **1.23**
- Look, listen and draw. **2.56**
- Game: *Stop the clock!*
- Rhyme: *Choose*

I don't touch.

Unit 7 · Lesson 8

Make a monster!

1

2

Key language:
monster

- Warm up
- Spelling
- Rhyme: *Art* **1.26**
- Make a monster.
- Game: *Choose*
- Rhyme: *Incy Wincy spider* **1.69**

3

4

Unit 8 • Lesson 1

A lovely sandcastle

Key language:
point; flag; Which (one) is yours?; (The) ... one; This/That one.

- Warm up
- Seek and say: *oi* **3.2**
- Rhyme: *Letters and sounds* **1.28**
- Read, listen and match. **3.3**
- Game: *Which one?*
- Rhyme: *Let's all go to the beach today!* **3.4**

oi

Unit 8 · Lesson 2

Treasure hunt

Key language:
treasure; spade; dig; beach

- Warm up
- Seek and say: *ure* **3.5**
- Rhyme: *Sounds* **1.32**
- Listen and answer. **3.6**
- Game: *Treasure bingo!*
- Rhyme: *Where's my teddy?* **3.7**

ure

Unit 8 • Lesson 3

Are they the same?

Key language:
starfish; crab; lobster; The others are ... ; (the) same/different shape/size/colour

- Warm up
- Hide and seek: *Mystery number*
- Rhyme: *Ways to make ten* **3.8**
- Look, listen and say. **3.9**
- Game: *Fish*
- Rhyme: *Colours (V1–3)* **2.2**

Unit 8 · Lesson 4

How many left?

Key language:
if; take .... away; How many are left?

- Warm up
- Hide and seek: *Mystery number*
- Rhyme: *There is one fish.* **3.10**
- Look, listen and count. **3.11**
- Game and Rhyme: *Round the seaweed!* **3.12**
- Rhyme: *How many left?* **3.13**

Unit 8 • Lesson 5

Who am I?

Key language:
beak; neck; gull; flamingo; rocks

- Warm up
- Letters and sounds
- Rhyme: *Our world* **1.17**
- Listen and stick. **3.14**
- Game: *Robot says*
- Rhyme: *Twenty legs* **1.40**

Unit 8 · Lesson 6

Looking at sand

Key language:
sand; sticks together; lump (n); stays the same shape; pours (v)

- Warm up
- Letters and sounds
- Rhyme: *Our world* **1.17**
- Read, listen and circle. **3.15**
- Game: *My pet*
- Rhyme: *Textures (V1–2)* **2.55**

1

wet dry

2

wet dry

3

wet dry

4

wet dry

Unit 8 • Lesson 7

Think of others

Key language:
plastic bag; seal; kill; spoil

- Warm up
- Reading
- Rhyme: *Values* **1.23**
- Read and match.
- Game: *Stop the clock!*
- Rhyme: *Choose*

Glass can cut.

Plastic can kill.

Rubbish spoils the beach.

I don't spoil the beach for others.

Unit 8 · Lesson 8

An underwater picture

1

2

3

4

Key language:
shake; sprinkle; tap (v); extra; underwater scene

- Warm up
- Spelling
- Rhyme: *Art* **1.26**
- Glue and sprinkle.
- Game: *Choose*
- Rhyme: *Let's all go to the beach today!* **3.4**

Unit 9 • Lesson 1

Help the farmer

Key language:
cow; hen; egg; milk (v); wife; keep clean

- Warm up
- Seek and say: *ow* **3.16**
- Rhyme: *Letters and sounds* **1.28**
- Listen, read and answer. **3.17**
- Game: *Help out!*
- Rhyme: *Uncle Ali has a farm.* **2.18**

ow

Unit 9 · Lesson 2

In the barn

Key language:
horse; barn; hay; Don't be afraid.; Don't forget ... ; inside; outside; afterwards

- Warm up
- Seek and say: *or* **3.18**
- Rhyme: *Sounds* **1.32**
- Listen and stick. **3.19**
- Game: *Don't do that!*
- Rhyme: *Horsey, horsey!* **3.20**

or

Unit 9 • Lesson 3

Doubles

Key language:
... add ... ; double

- Warm up
- Hide and seek: *Mystery number*
- Rhyme: *Ways to make ten* **3.8**
- Listen and match. **3.21**
- Game: *Double up*
- Rhyme: *Doubles* **3.22**

Unit 9 • Lesson 4
Which holds the most?

Key language:
full; half-full; empty; ... holds the most; ... holds the least

- Warm up
- Hide and seek: *Mystery number*
- Rhyme: *How many left?* **3.13**
- Listen, read and answer. **3.23**
- Game: *Whose holds the most?*
- Rhyme: *There's a hole in my bucket.* **3.24**

60 70 80 90 100

Unit 9 · Lesson 5

Farm animals

Key language:

We get … from … ;
… give us … ; also; buy

- Warm up
- Letters and sounds
- Rhyme: *Our world* **1.17**
- Stick, listen and match. **3.25**
- Game: *On the farm*
- Rhyme: *Baa, baa, black sheep* **3.26**

What do we get from … ?

goats

sheep

milk

wool

eggs

cows

hens

Unit 9 · Lesson 6

Floating and sinking

What do you think?

1

2

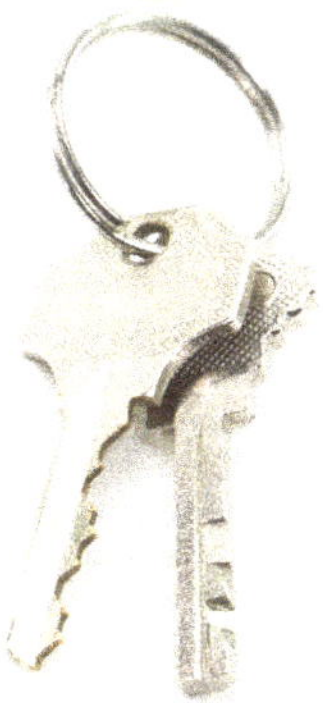

3

4

float

or

sink?

Key language:
float; sink; test (v); (be) surprised

- Warm up
- Letters and sounds
- Rhyme: *Our world* **1.17**
- Watch and match.
- Game: *Mime*
- Rhyme: *Chick, chick, chick, chick, chicken* **3.27**

Unit 9 • Lesson 7

Happy and healthy

Key language:
shelter (n); medicine; healthy (well)

- Warm up
- Reading
- Rhyme: *Values* **1.23**
- Listen and stick. **3.28**
- Game: *Stop the clock!*
- Rhyme: *Choose*

I know what animals need.

Unit 9 · Lesson 8

A farmyard picture

1

2

Key language:

farmyard

- Warm up
- Spelling
- Rhyme: *Art* **1.26**
- Design and make.
- Game: *Choose*
- Rhyme: *The farmer's on his farm.* **3.29**

3

4

Unit 10 • Lesson 1

In the morning

Key language:
ear; get washed/dressed; have breakfast; go to school; before; after

- Warm up
- Seek and say: *ear* **3.30**
- Rhyme: *Letters and sounds* **1.28**
- Listen and answer. **3.31**
- Game: *Robot says*
- Rhyme: *Coming to school (V1–2)* **1.55**

ear

Unit 10 · Lesson 2
After school

Key language:
night; have a rest; visit; That's (not) right!; supper; Goodnight!

- Warm up
- Seek and say: *igh* **3.32**
- Rhyme: *Sounds* **1.32**
- Listen and answer. **3.33**
- Game: *What's missing?*
- Rhyme: *Twinkle, twinkle little star!* **3.34**

igh

Unit 10 · Lesson 3

Home time

Key language:
lunchtime; home time; snack time; line up

- Warm up
- Hide and seek: *Mystery number*
- Rhyme: *Doubles* **3.22**
- Read and listen. **3.35**
- Game: *What's next?*
- Rhyme: *Coming to school (V1–3)* **3.36**

1

2

Unit 10 · Lesson 4
It's time for ...

Key language:
When's (lunch)?; It can't be (time for bed yet!)

- Warm up
- Hide and seek: *Mystery number*
- Rhyme: *Ways to make ten* **3.8**
- Listen and draw. **3.37**
- Game: *This is my day.*
- Rhyme: *Hop round the clock!* **1.60**

Unit 10 · Lesson 5

Keeping fit

Key language:
exercise; feel good/well; active

- Warm up
- Letters and sounds
- Rhyme: *Our world* **1.17**
- Look and stick.
- Game: *Mime*
- Rhyme: *My body (V1–3)* **3.38**

1

2

3

Are they being active?

4

5

6

Unit 10 · Lesson 6

Healthy teeth

Key language:
tooth; toothbrush; toothpaste; smile

- Warm up
- Letters and sounds
- Rhyme: *Our world* 1.17
- Look and tick.
- Game: *Odd one out*
- Rhyme: *Wash (V1–4)* 3.39

Good or bad for your teeth?

Unit 10 • Lesson 7
On time

Key language:
late; on time; miss the bus; glad

- Warm up
- Reading
- Rhyme: *Values* **1.23**
- Look and draw.
- Game: *Stop the clock!*
- Rhyme: *Coming to school* *(V1–3)* **3.36**

I am on time.

Are they on time?

Unit 10 · Lesson 8

My name

1

2

3

4

Key language:
straw; twig; (lolly) stick (n); stripes

- Warm up
- Spelling
- Rhyme: *Art* **1.26**
- Design and make.
- Game: *Choose*
- Rhyme: *I know the alphabet!* **3.40**

oo

book zoo

th

three this

ar

car

ch

chip

er

teacher

ee

feet

oi

point

ure

treasure

ow

cow

oa

boat

ng

swing

ai

paint

air

hair

sh

fish

ur

fur

or

horse

ear

ear

igh

night

Pupil's Book 3 Sight words

1.1 here	1.1 I	1.2 don't	1.3 isn't
2.1 your	2.2 you	3.1 by	3.3 to
3.6 my	3.7 do	4.3 very	4.3 which
4.3 yours	4.5 warm	4.6 make	5.1 please

5.1 she's	5.2 he's	5.4 above	5.6 first
5.7 time	6.3 they're	6.4 more	8.1 little
8.1 one	9.3 all	9.3 white	9.4 so
9.4 when			

CENGAGE Learning

Hide and Seek Pupil's Book 3, 1st Edition

Jane Thompson and Stephen Thompson

Publisher: Sharon Jervis

Commissioning Editor: Carol Goodwright

Development Editor: Carol Goodwright

Content Project Manager: Jon Ricketts

Manufacturing Buyer: Elaine Field

Head of Strategic Marketing – ELT: Charlotte Ellis

Design and Composition: Tighe | SPi Global

The authors and publisher would like to thank the following for their collaboration on this project:

Consultants and Readers:

Jennifer Heath, ELT author and consultant, Europe; David A. Hill, ELT author and consultant, Europe; Luciana Verónica Fernández, Early Literacy Specialist and Teacher Trainer, Argentina; Tom Kelley, Educational Consultant, Cengage Learning, UAE; Sondos Fakhr El Deen, Kingdom of Saudi Arabia; Yuta Otake, Cambodia; Estrelita Maria Gaspar, Singapore; Ann Han, China; Huynh Thuy Thuy Linh, Vietnam; Sylvia Goddard, UK, Suzanne Cummings, UK.

Illustrators:

6, 12, 15, 22–23, 31, 36, 39, 44, 55, 60–61, 76–77, David Harston; 4–5, 13, 20, 30, 38, 45, 47, 54, 62–63, 78–79, Jason Wolff; 7, 14, 21, 28–29, 37, 46, 52–53, 68– 71, Joseph W. Ewers; 10, 18, 26, 34, 42, 50, 58, 82 Julissa Mora

Recordings: Recorded in London by John Green TEFL Audio. Music for the songs and chants composed and arranged by Tim Woolf.

Commissioned photos: Richard Brown (www.richardbrownphotographer.com)

Photo Credits: All images sourced from Shutterstock unless otherwise stated:

8 (tl) Vlad61; **8 (tr bkgd)** LittleMiss; **8 (tr)** Ixpert; **8 (bl)** Olga_i; **8 (br)** Sergey Novikov; **9 (tl)** Svitlana-ua; **9 (tr)** Olesya Feketa; **9 (bl)** Digital Fabiani; **9 (br)** Daniel Rodriguez/iStockphoto; **10 (t)** Kostenyukova Nataliya; **16 (tl)** Ivan Feoktistov; **16 (tr)** Rebell; **16 (b)** Helen E. Grose; **17 (tl)** Neil Hardwick; **17 (bl)** Nattanan726; **17 (r)** Becky Sheridan; **17 (bkgd)** David M. Schrader; **25 (t)** Viacheslav Nikolaenko; **25 (bl)** Pecold; **25 (br)** Maxim Tupikov; **32 (l)** ZouZou; **32 (tr)** Jeka; **32 (br)** Eric Isselee; **33 (r)** Paleka; **34 (t)** Kostenyukova Nataliya; **40 (bl)** Goodluz; **40 (t)** Monkey Business Images; **40 (br)** StockLite; **41 (bl)** Ikonoklast Fotografie; **41 (br)** Ikonoklast Fotografie; **41 (tl)** Ikonoklast Fotografie; **41 (tr)** Ikonoklast Fotografie; **48 (tl)** Jorg Hackemann; **48 (tc)** Kuttelvaserova Stuchelova; **48 (tr)** Zurijeta; **48 (bl)** Mariyana M; **48 (bc)** Stuart Jenner; **48 (br)** Lawrence Manning/Corbis; **49 (tl)** An Nguyen; **49 (bl)** Shvaygert Ekaterina; **49 (tr)** GoodMood Photo; **49 (br)** Oleksiy Mark; **50 (r)** Kostenyukova Nataliya; **56 (bkgd)** Naypong; **57 (bl; tr)** LeonP; **57 (bc; tl)** Stefan Pircher; **57 (br; tc)** Chris Hill; **64 (bkgd)** Gabriele Maltinti; **65 (tl)** Nestor Bandrivskyy; **65 (tr)** Yory Frenklakh; **65 (bl)** Leigh Prather; **65 (br)** Ozerov Alexander; **66 (bkgd)** Pakhnyushchy; **66 (bl)** Fabien Monteil; **66 (tl)** Ever; **66 (r)** David J. Martin; **72 (tl, tc, bl)** Eric Isselee; **72 (tr)** G.K. & Vikki Hart/Photodisc/Getty Images; **72 (br)** Valentina_S; **72 (bc)** Tsekhmister; **73 (tl)** Maxim_Kovalev; **73 (tcl)** Little Stocker; **73 (tcr)** Dima Sobko; **73 (tr)** Denis Nata; **73 (b)** Yeryomina Anastassiya; **74 (tl)** Sari Oneal; **74 (tr)** Catalin Petolea; **74 (bl)** Itakefotos4u; **74 (br)** Monkey Business Images; **80 (tl)** Monkey Business Images; **80 (tc)** Greenland; **80 (tr)** Stefanolunardi; **80 (bl)** Sakkmesterke; **80 (bc)** Gorilla Images; **80 (br)** Sergey Novikov; **81 (cl)** Omni Art; **81 (tl)** Vorobyeva; **81 (cr)** M. Unal Ozmen; **81 (tr)** Violetkaipa; **81 (b)** V. S. Anandhakrishna; **82 (tc, tr, bc, br)** Kostenyukova Nataliya.

Sticker Photo Credits:

22 (station) Wizdata; **22 (taxi)** Art Konovalov; **22 (bus)** Andrey Armyagov; **24 (road)** Concept Photo; **24 (boat)** Zhu Difeng; **24 (train)** Alysta; **33 (paint)** Beth Swanson; **56 (polar bear)** Olga_gl; **56 (turtle)** Neophuket; **56 (hedgehog)** Eric Isselee; **64 (flamingo)** James Steidl; **64 (crab)** Nicholas Toh; **64 (starfish)** Allocricetulus; **64 (bird)** Eric Isselee; **72 (milk)** Jiri Hera; **72 (eggs)** Jiang Hongyan; **72 (wool)** Meelis Endla; **Smiley face** Patimat Alieva.

Printed in the United Kingdom by Ashford Colour Press Ltd

Print Number: 06 Print Year: 2023

For product information and technology assistance, contact **emea.info@cengage.com**.

For permission to use material from this text or product, and for permission queries, email **emea.permissions@cengage.com.**

British Library Cataloguing-in-Publication Data
A catalogue record for this book is available from the British Library.

ISBN: 978-1-408-06251-7

Cengage Learning EMEA
Cheriton House, North Way, Andover, Hampshire, SP10 5BE United Kingdom

Cengage Learning products are represented in Canada by Nelson Education Ltd.

For your lifelong learning solutions, visit **www.cengage.co.uk**

MIX Paper from responsible sources FSC® C011748 www.fsc.org

Unit 1, page 8

skip | run | jump | swim

Unit 1, page 9

Jon | Kim | Dan | Tess

Unit 2, page 14

ca__

6

Unit 2, page 17

racoon

moth

fox

Unit 3, page 20

bus

car

Unit 3, page 22

Unit 4, page 28

Bring | swing

Unit 5

Jim | Max | Alex

Unit 3, page 24

Unit 4, page 33

Unit 6, page 45

chair | feel

Unit 6, page 47

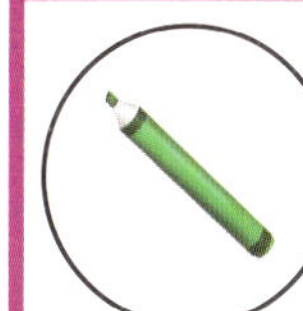
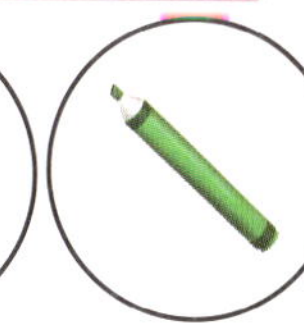

Unit 7, page 55